Śiva Mahimna Stotram-Tika

Śiva Mahiṁna Stotram-Tika

by Madhusūdana Sarasvati

Translated into English

KRISHNAJEE AYYAGARI

Motilal Banarsidass Publications

MOTILAL BANARSIDASS
PUBLICATIONS
4741/23, Ansari Road, Daryaganj, New Delhi - 110002 (India)
Email: *mlbd@mlbd.com* | *sales@mlbd.com* | *exports@mlbd.com*
Website: *www.mlbd.com*

Śiva Mahiṁna Stotram-Tika
by
Krishnajee Ayyagari

First Edition Published in 2022

Published in India by Motilal Banarsidass Publications

ISBN : 978-93-91759-24-7 (PB)

Printed and bound in India

Foreword

Stotra literature origins from the Vedas and expands in a vast field. Some stotras are considered as Stotra Kāvyas i.e., poems in the form of hymns. Śiva Mahiṁna stotra – one of the earliest stotra kāvyas attained a special status among the stotras and being a factor of mesmerizing for the devotees of lord Śiva. The hymns are considered to have magical power and the stotra is considered as Mantratmaka – an embodiment of magic syllables. Like Saundarya Lahari of Ādi Śaṅkara, this stotra possesses the state of a hymn, stotra, and poetry. Puṣpadanta, a celestial being is attributed as the author of this stotra, and the legends therein are known hereditarily. The Mahimana stotras have their impact from these stotras and we have so many stotras like Saktimahimna stotra, Ganesa mahimnaḥ stotra, etc.

Madhusūdana Sarasvatī, an authentic exponent of Advaita Vedānta and a great devotee of Lord Kṛṣṇa wrote a commentary for this great stotra kāvya and interpreted the verses also to fit for lord Kṛṣṇa, thus making his view Hari-Harābheda-Advaitic one. The poetry has a lucid style of poetry and it attracts the reader with all its eloquence.

These kinds of attempts may be the inspiration behind the worship of the deity Shankar Narayana, a combined deity form of Shiva (Shankara) on the right with Nandi and Vishnu (Narayana) on the left with Garuda. A temple for Shankaranarayana is situated in Shankaranarayana village, named after the temple, which is in the valley of mountain ranges close to the Sahyadri's. It is in Udupi District, Karnataka. The names Shankararama, Ramasubrahmanya are well known in southern parts of India. Even the Carnatic lyrics Ma Ramanan Uma Ramanan hails this tradition

It gives immense pleasure to note that Krishnajee Ayyagari has translated this great work into English with its original flavour. The translation is elegant and appreciable. This one seems to be the first attempt of its kind and I feel that this effort should be appreciated by the entire Sanskrit fraternity. Culling out the rare things in Sanskrit and translating them into English is the need of the hour since that alone possesses a message to the younger generation to motivate towards this great language and culture.

I deem it a great honor and a matter of pride to give a foreword to this translation and I request all the readers to go through the same and to appreciate the efforts taken by the author. The appreciation would provide a great motivation among the scholars to bring forth the rare and hidden marvels of Sanskrit into the new generation. I pray to the Almighty to give a healthy life and energy to the author to come up with more such brilliant ideas and to serve the Surabhāratī.

Dr. Satheesha K.S
Professor and Head of Dept,
Department of Vedanta
National Sanskrit University
Tirupati Andhra Pradesh

Acknowledgments

I am glad to mention that some of my friends and well-wishers who read my Book "Bhakti- A critical appraisal of Madhusūdana Sarasvati" enquired about the source of the books authored by Madhusūdana Sarasvati and suggested translating the full text of Mahimnastotra tika into English. Inspired by their suggestion I have attempted to do this work.

I have forwarded the draft of my translation to learned professors for their views and requested their review.

Dr. Satheesha K.S, Prof. and Head of the department of Advaita Vedanta, at Sanskrit University, Tirupati. A.P. (India) has, despite his preoccupation with prior commitments. spared time to go through the draft and wrote a befitting foreword to the book. I wholeheartedly offer my thanks.

Dr. Satchitānanda Mishra, presently member secretary of ICPR New Delhi, and Dr. Ananda Mishra, Prof, and Head of the Department of Philosophy and Religion, BHU, Varanasi extended their support and encouragement when I was a research scholar at BHU, Varanasi. Despite their busy work schedules and preoccupations, they have obliged my request to go through the draft and have written crisp reviews on the work. I offer my respects and thanks to them.

Sri Subramanian V, (popularly known as Subbu Ji), a former official at RBI has in-depth knowledge of the Sanskrit language and Sankara Vedanta literature and is an active senior participant in the Advaita Google group discussions. My sincere thanks for his suggestions and for writing a lucid review on the book.

I am indebted to Dr, R.K, Jha, Professor in Philosophy who was my supervisor and guide for my Doctoral study at BHU Varanasi. He is an ideal teacher who, with his in-depth knowledge of Vedanta Philosophy, made me learn methodically from the basics and obtain my Ph.D. He has encouraged me to publish a book based on my thesis. I owe my highest regard and respect to him.

My appreciation and thanks to Sri Rajeev Jain of Motilal Banarsidass Publications in New Delhi for agreeing to publish the work. I also appreciate the effort of Mrs. Manju Arya in getting the cover design and the speeding up publication with keen interest

Krishnajee Ayyagari.

Review

There are many classical hymns in the Bharatiya sampradaya. One among them is the 'Shiva Mahimnastotra' which is also referred to as 'Mahiṁnastotra'. It is popularly held that the work was authored by a Gandharva known as Pushpadanta. Of the several verses in this text, the one that inspires the lofty idea of 'oneness' among the different schools such as Vaishnavism, Shaivism, Patanjali's Yoga, etc., is this:

अतीतः पन्थानं तव च महिमा वाङ्मनसयो –
रतव्द्यावृत्त्या यं चकितमभिधत्ते श्रुतिरपि ।
स कस्य स्तोतव्यः कतिविधगुणः कस्य विषयः
पदे त्वर्वाचीने पतति न मनः कस्य न वचः ॥२॥

Your greatness is beyond the reach of mind and speech. Who can properly praise that which even the Vedas describe with trepidation, by means of 'neti-neti / not this, not this? 'How many qualities does He possess? By whom can He be perceived?' Yet whose mind and speech do not turn to the (saguna) form later taken by Him?

From this one sample, we are able to appreciate the great Vedantic purport of this text.

Here is one more. In the 30th verse Pushpadanta says:

बहलरजसे विश्वोत्पत्तौ भवाय नमो नमः
प्रबलतमसे तत्संहारे हराय नमो नमः ।
जनसुखकृते सत्त्वोद्रिक्तौ मृडाय नमो नमः
प्रमहसि पदे निस्त्रैगुण्ये शिवाय नमो नमः ॥३०॥

Salutations to You as Brahma, in whom rajas prevail for the creation of the universe. Salutations to You as Rudra, in whom tamas prevails for its destruction. Salutations to You as Vishnu, in whom sattva prevails for giving happiness to the people. Salutations to You, O Shiva, who is effulgent and beyond the three attributes. (30)

In this verse, Brahman is praised as the One entity beyond the three Guṇas, who alone creates, protects, and annihilates the universe by taking up the three gunas, as the Trimurti-s

Sri Madhusūdana Saraswathi, the great Advaitin, has commented on this text in a unique way: He has seen each verse as a depiction of Hara, Shiva, and Hari, Narayana. Even though widely known as an ardent Krishna bhakta, Sri Madhusūdana Saraswathi takes up the task of commenting on the Mahimna stotra by looking at the hymn as praise of Hari and Hara. This indeed is a very great contribution to Bhartiya bhakti literature. The author's zeal in bringing out the Hari-Hara abheda, is non-difference, as can be seen in his concluding verses at the end of the commentary.

हररशंकरयोरभेदबोधो भवितु क्षुद्रधियामपीति यत्नात् ।
उभयार्थतया मयेदमुक्तं सुधियः साधुतयैव शोधयन्तु ॥१॥

[With the benediction that the understanding of non-difference between Hari and Sankara may arise even in those with a lowly intellect have I, with effort, commented on the Sivmahiṁna stotra verses in dual-meaning mode (as applying to Hari and Hara). Let the noble ones accept this as admissible alone.]

भूतिभूषितदेहाय द्विजराजेन राजते ।
एकात्मने नमो नित्यं हरये च हराय च ॥

Obeisance ever to Him, who is resplendent with His body adorned with vibhūti, ashes, and is of the complexion of camphor (or having the moon on His head), the One Atman that is both Hara and Hari.

Sri Krishnajee Ayyagari, the author of the rendering of this text, along with the commentary of Madhusūdana Saraswathi, to English, has put in his efforts to bring out the salient points of the original. This translation is bound to benefit many a true seeker.

Om Tat Sat
Sri V. Subramanian
Advaita Philosopher,
(Formerly Officer in RBI)

Dr. Krishna ji Ayyagiri is a devoted scholar. He completed his Ph.D. in his eighties. He is a true vidyānurāgī. After completing his research and getting the thesis published in book form, he is now publishing this book with his own English translation of the commentary written by Madhusūdana Sarasvati on the Śiva Mahiṁna Stotram.

The commentary by Madhusūdana Sarasvati on Śiva Mahiṁna Stotram is significant work. This Stotra is a very popular prayer among the devotees of Lord Śiva in India. Almost in every temple of Lord Śiva, this prayer is recited. This stotra contains 45 slokas. It is believed that this stotra was composed by a Gandharva as an apology prayer for the mistakes he committed unintentionally.

The name of Madhusūdana Sarasvati needs no introduction to any serious student of Indian Philosophy. He wrote many important books on Vedānta philosophy. Besides being a great scholar of Advaita philosophy he was also a great Bhakta.

The commentary written by Madhusūdana Sarasvati on this text is unique in the sense that the commentator has presented two alternative meanings of each sloka wherein one meaning is applicable to Lord Śiva and the other one is applicable to Lord Vishnu. Madhusūdana Sarasvati is a very humble scholar despite having a deep understanding of Advaita philosophy and all the schools of Indian philosophy in general. The real intention of writing such a commentary was to show that there is no difference between these two, the Lord Śiva and the Lord Vishnu. One is free to worship any deity of his choice.

This is a famous statement" ***Sarvadevanamaskarah keshavam Prati gacchati***", bowing/worship to any God reaches to Lord Vishnu. Therefore, a true student of Advaita philosophy never hates any God as for him every God is only vyāvahārika not pāramārthika. God is only an instrument to achieve liberation, to realize the nature of self, where one must concentrate his mind. God, the preceptor and the pupil all the three are identical, however, they are empirically different.

ईश्वरो गुरुरात्मेति मूर्तिभेदविभागिने।
व्योमवदव्याप्तदेहाय दक्षिणामूर्तये नमः।।

is the unique prayer in Advaita tradition. A philosophy which doesn't accept a difference even between the teacher and the taught, between God and the Jīvātman, how could accept a difference between two gods?

Dr Ayyagiri has rightly pointed it out in the introduction:

"The purpose of writing the commentary is laudable as it aims to clarify that there is no difference between Śiva and Viṣṇu especially the inter religious wrangles prevailing during his time and several people propagating different Gods and claiming that their deity is superior to others and misguiding the innocent people. The confusion and tension by these interreligious wrangles is so severe than even by the alien religions. Madhusūdana Sarasvati conveyed the essence of the following.

Śivāya viṣṇurūpāya, viṣṇurūpāya Śivaah."

What Dr. Ayyagiri has stated regarding Madhusūdana Sarasvati is also true regarding Ācārya Shankara. He wrote commentaries on Gīta and also on Vishnu sahasra Nama. On the one hand he writes Daśaśloki in which he clearly propounds that ***tadeko'vashistah shivah kevalo'ham*** and on the other he writes the prayer ***Bhaja Govindam mūdhamate***.

The position of Madhusūdana Sarasvati is completely in tune with Ācārya Shankara. Ācārya Shankara is a great unifier of Hinduism. As all the rivers go to the ocean in the same way all the philosophies merge in the Advaita philosophy. It will not be far away from reality if I say that the Advaita philosophy is the chief current of Hindu thought.

Dr. Ayyagiri has done a wonderful job in translating this significant work into English and publishing it for the people who are not comfortable in Sanskrit. I have gone through the translation and found the translation dependable and true to the spirit of the original text. I congratulate Dr. Ayyagiri for this work and wish him to do some more such works as such types of works are a kind of worship

Dr. Satchitānanda Mishra
Member Secretary, ICPR,
New Delhi.
(Prof in Sanskrit, BHU Varanasi)

It was really a blissful experience for me to read the Shivamahimnastotram of Pushpadanta with commentary of Madhusūdana Sarasvati which is translated in English by Dr. Krishnajee Ayyagari. Several editions have come out in recent past of Shivamahimnastotra which is one of the best devotional hymns written in praise of the Almighty God Shiva or Hara. Now the beauty of this commentary is that it skillfully shown that the hymns dedicated to Shiva are equally applicable Vishnu.

The commentator has with authority of scriptures established that the aspirant can chose any deity of his choice and adopt any path as per his ability and attitude and all will reach the same destination, like all rivers ultimately reach and merge in the Ocean. This is the major contribution of the present text.

This is the typical synthetic and harmonious approach. God is the same whether he is called Ishvara, Allah or God. This was the view of Ramakrishna Paramahaṁsa and Vivekananda who were the people who popularized the concept to the masses globally. Keeping in view the spirit of this approach Dr. Krishnajee Ayyagari who is scholar of Bhakti and Religious consciousness has taken pains by carefully translating the Original Sanskrit commentary of Madhusūdana Sarasvati into English. I congratulate Krishnajee for his commendable effort.

Prof. Ananda Mishra
Prof and Head,
Department of Philosophy and Religion
BHU Varanasi UP.

Śiva Mahiṁna Stotram - Tika

by Madhusūdana Sarasvati

Slokas in Sanskrit - A translation in English

Introduction:

The Mahiṁna Stotra is a very popular prayer among the devotees of Siva in India and is recited and translated in several Indian languages.

Mahiṁna stotra is a Sanskrit text containing slokas in Praise of Lord Siva which was believed to have been composed extempore by a Gandharva seeking pardon for his mistakes committed by him inadvertently.

The legend of the story is as follows:

Puṣpadanta (literally means one with flowerlike teeth) was a Gandharva, a celestial musician. In Hindu puranic stories there are celestials called Yaksha (archangels), Kinnar (nymphs), Gandharva (musicians) and Apsara (celestial dancers) etc. who are are said to serve in the court of Indra (the king of celestial kingdom). They are in contact with the higher plane that of the Gods. They have some mystical powers like invisibility to human eyes and are superior to humans and have ability to fly in celestial atmosphere, but not equivalent to angels or Gods.

A King named Chitraratha was a devotee of Lord Śiva. The king has established a big garden adorned with various types of fragrant flowers with beautiful colors. The King used to offer flowers from his garden as a part of his daily morning devotional prayers to Lord Śiva.

Puṣpadanta is the king of the clan of Gandharvas. He was also a devotee of Lord Śiva and a lover of flowers. He has one day chanced to see the garden with beautiful flowers. He was so much enchanted that he could not control his emotions and picked up the flowers from the garden thanking himself for the opportunity of offering so many beautiful varieties of flowers to his deity Śiva.

In the morning when the gardener went to pick the flowers, he was surprised not finding any flowers. The matter was humbly reported to the King, as a result, King Chitraratha was left with no flowers to complete his prayers to Lord Śiva.

Puṣpadanta was so much enchanted with the flowers that he continued to visit the garden regularly and pick the flowers. The personnel engaged to guard the garden could not find out any clue as to how the flowers are missing despite tight vigilance. The King did all he could to address the issue and finally thought of a novel idea to solve this problem.

He ordered to spread Nirmālya (Bilva leaves offered to the Lord on the previous day) in the paths of the garden. The Nirmālya is considered very sacred and anybody trampling them will face the wrath of the Lord.

Puṣpadanta was unaware of this and stepped on the Bilva leaves. This infuriated Lord Śiva and he punished Puṣpadanta by taking away his divine powers. He immediately realized that some grave sin has been committed by him and started to pray to the Lord in expiation of his sin committed unknowingly. Lord Śiva, was pleased with his prayers, absolved him of the mistake and restored his divine powers. This prayer became well known as the 'Śiva Mahiṁna Stotra'.

The legend says that this stotra was inscribed on the walls of the sanctorum of the famous dwadasa Jyothir linga Amaralingeśwara temple at Omkareswara (near Indore) in Madhyapradesh state of India some time in 1063AD.This is perhaps the oldest available proof of this stotra.

The stotra contains 45 slokas and the thirty seventh sloka confirms that the stotra was composed by Puṣpadanta.

Mr. Norman Brown has authored a book entitled **The Mahimnastava or Praise of Śiva's Greatness** "published by The American Institute of Indian Studies, Poona in 1964, and republished by Motilal Banarasidas, New Delhi in 1983. He has collected historical records from various sources.

i) Baroda Museum which contained 36 stanzas along with miniature paintings.

ii) India office Library, London which contains 37 slokas.

iii) Manuscripts from McGill University Museum Montreal which contains 42 stanzas

iv) University of Pennsylvania (USA) which contain 43 stanzas

Mr. NormanBrown also mentioned that there are three printed versions published in 1937, 1953 and 1954 with different number of stanzas etc.

The book of Arthur Avalon in English published by Ganesh and company, Madras (1953 edition, first published in 1916 which is out of print now). It contains the commentary of Sanskrit pundit Jagannadha Chakravartī. and translated by Arthur Avalon and contains only 35 verses.

Norman Brown has confirmed that the commentary of Madhusūdana Sarasvati treats only 31 stanzas. So, the stanzas from 32 on words might have been added subsequently mostly describing the benefits of reciting or listening to this stotra.

The first 23 slokas are devoted praising the lord for the fulfillment of desires and in the next seven slokas are dedicated to motiveless devotion which is of higher order. The stotra has praised the Lord in both Saguṇa Swarūpa (God with attributes) and Nirguṇa Swarūpa (without attributes).

The concluding stanzas of the stotra describes the benefits of reciting or even listening to the stotra as follows.

"Anyone who recites this hymn with a pure heart and devotion will be blessed with fame, wealth, long life and virtuous children in this mortal world, and attain Kailas (Śiva's abode) after death. Benefit of singing Shivmahiṁna stotra is far greater than either the benefit of spiritual initiation, charity, austerity, pilgrimage, knowledge of the scriptures or the performance of ceremonial Yagnas."

The present publication is a translation of the commentary written by Madhusūdana Sarasvati.

Śrī Madhusūdana Sarasvatī is one of the prominent Advaita Philosopher who has composed great works like Advaita Siddhi, Bhaktirasāyana etc. has written a unique commentary in Sanskrit. The commentary is unique in that it was written in a dual way, one in favor of Śiva as per the text and the commentary equally applicable in favor of Viṣṇu or His incarnations. He has shown literary skills in Sanskrit and his proficiency and knowledge of Vedas and scriptures. His commentary on stanza 7 is considered as a separate work called '**Prasthānabheda**' for some time and published in as a small booklet.

Madhusūdana Sarasvati has also stated that he has taken pains to make it clear that a devotee can chose to worship any deity of his choice and there is no distinction between Śiva and Viṣṇu and this should be known by all, and the learned people will accept this as acceptable.

The purpose of writing the commentary is laudable as it aims to clarify that there is no difference between Śiva and Viṣṇu especially the inter religious wrangles prevailing during his time and several people propagating different Gods and claiming that their deity is superior to others and misguiding the innocent people. The confusion and tension by these interreligious wrangles is so severe than even by the the alien religions.

Madhusūdana Sarasvati conveyed the essence of the following.

Śivāya viṣṇurūpāya, viṣṇurūpāya Śivaah.

There is also a legend that Viṣṇu has told the following.

"*Madbhakto Śivadveṣi, maddveṣi sankarapriya narakyanthi ācandradivākaram*" meaning that the devotees of Viṣṇu who hate Lord Śiva and those devotees of Śiva who hate Viṣṇu, all such people are deemed to have committed unpardonable sin that they will go to hell as long as Sun and Moon exists, that means they will eternally remain in hell.

The following books have been consulted in doing the translation.

i) Mahimnastotra Śrī Madhusūdana Sarasvatī tika-tadardha bhashānuvada sahitam in Hindi, By Pandit Rala Rama sarma, Published by Choukambha Vidyābhavan, Varanasi, 2001.

ii) Śrī Puṣpadanta virachita Śrī Shivmahiṁna stotram Śrī Madhusūdana Sarasvati krutha Vyākhyā Andhra tātparyam vivaraṇa sahitam in Telugu by Śrī Kasi kshetra nivāsi Śrī Jñānanada Teertha swami. Published by Vavilla Ramaswamy Śāstrulu and sons, Chennapuri. 1939. (This does not contain the commentary in favor of Viṣṇu.)

iii) Śrī Gandharva raja Puṣpadanta virachita Mahiṁnastotra. A commentary in Telugu by Dr. R. Lakshmana Moorthy and Prof S. Laxman Murty. A private publication from Warangal.

There is no translation of the commentary of Madhusūdana Sarasvati in English to the best of my knowledge and enquiry. To bring the same to a larger public a humble effort is made to translate into English. This is a freelance translation.

॥ अथ श्री शिवमम्निस्तोत्रम् ॥

atha śrī śivamahimnaḥ stotraṁ

Verse 1

महिम्नः पारं ते परमविदुषो यद्यसदृशी
स्तुतिर्ब्रह्मादीनामपि तदवसन्नास्त्वयि गिरः।
अथाऽवाच्यः सर्वः स्वमतिपरिमाणावधि गृणन्
ममाप्येष स्तोत्रे हर निरपवादः परिकरः॥ १॥

mahimnaḥ pāraṁ te parāmaviduṣo yadyasadṛśī
stutirbrahmādīnāmapi tadavasannāstvayi giraḥ |
athā'vācyaḥ sarvaḥ svamatiparimāṇāvadhi gṛṇan
mamāpyeṣa stotre hara nirapavādaḥ parikaraḥ || 1 ||

1 (a) Meaning and Explanation:

Mahadeva!

The sloka addressed as ' ***Hara*** ' meaning the Supreme Lord is that who would destroy all grief and all sorts of sorrows arising out of ignorance.

The glory of the Lord is so immense that cannot be exhaustively described as there are innumerable infinite auspicious qualities that even wise people cannot apprehend adequately. Praise by ignorant people who are ignorant of the glories of the Lord may be infructuous. In such case the devotion of even divine personalities like Brahma may not be considered adequate. However, the praise by anybody who has grasped your glories to the extent of their capabilities is considered acceptable. In such a case my effort to praise you may be considered as relevant and acceptable.

1 (b) Applicable to Vishnu:

The same is applicable in favor of Viṣṇu. Hara means who destroys. Madhusūdana used his linguistic skill. If stotra hara is split as (Stotre + ahara), the word ahara means protector.

Thus Hara (Śiva) is the destroyer of misfortunes and Viṣṇu is the protector of Joy.

❩❩❩

Verse 2

अतीतः पंथानं तव च महिमा वाङ्मनसयोः
अतद्व्यावृत्त्या यं चकितमभिधत्ते श्रुतिरपि।
स कस्य स्तोतव्यः कतिविधगुणः कस्य विषयः
पदे त्वर्वाचीने पतति न मनः कस्य न वचः॥ २॥

atītaḥ paṁthānaṁ tava ca mahimā vāṅmanasayoḥ
atadvyāvṛttyā yaṁ cakitamabhidhatte śrutirapi |
sa kasya stotavyaḥ katividhaguṇaḥ kasya viṣayaḥ
pade tvarvācīne patati na manaḥ kasya na vacaḥ || 2 ||

2 (a) Meaning and Explanation:

O Śaṅkara! Your majesty and glory transcend all limits of expression and imagination. Even the great Vedas themselves are unequal to specifically describe in its entirety the nature and qualities of the unmanifest (attribute-less) form of the Lord called Nirguṇa Swarūpa It is not possible for anybody to estimate the limit less qualities of the Lord and comprehend the Nirguna Swaroopa of the Lord. The Lord has taken a new form with attributes (accompanied by His consort) due to compassion towards the devotees. Thus, everyone can perceive and sing the praises by which they can please the Lord.

The immense qualities and glories of the attribute-less form of the Lord (Nirguna) are beyond the scope of description by either expression or imagination by mind. Even the supreme scripture Vedas also could not specifically describe the self-luminous consciousness aspect of the Lord.

The Sagun Swarūpa is the same aspect of the Nirguṇa but with form and attributes which the Lord has taken out of compassion towards the devotees. The immense qualities of the Lord remaining the same can be described.

The new form of the Lord with five heads, three eyes, with Bhasma smeared over the body, attired in tiger skin, the cobra decorated on his neck as an ornament. His armaments are Pinaka, a conch, Khatvanga, and trisula are held in HIS four hands. He is accompanied by His consort Parvati, riding on a bull called Nandeśwar looks very enchanting to see. Thus, with the physically perceivable enchanting appearance before them no devotee either learned or lay, can desist from contemplating in mind and singing His praises in humility that will please the Lord.

Thus the devotee with dispassion who meditates on the Nirguṇa, and the devotee who worships the Saguna aspect will realize the Lord's glory.

2 (b) Explanation as applicable to Viṣṇu:

The Manifest form of Viṣṇu has an enchanting appearance with shy blue complexion of his body, a conch, the Sudarshan disc, mace (as armaments) and a Lotus flower held in his hands, decorated with glittering Kaustubh gem in his necklace, accompanied by His consort Lakshmi. A devout aspirant aspiring realization (a learned or a lay) cannot desist from singing His praises and visualizing His presence.

Verse 3

मधुस्फीता वाचः परममृतं निर्मितवतः
तव ब्रह्मन् किं वागपि सुरगुरोर्विस्मयपदम्।
मम त्वेतां वाणीं गुणकथनपुण्येन भवतः
पुनामीत्यर्थेऽस्मिन् पुरमथन बुद्धिर्व्यवसिता॥ ३॥

madhusphītā vācaḥ paRāmamṛtaṁ nirmitavataḥ
tava brahman kiṁ vāgapi suragurorvismayapadam |
mama tvetāṁ vāṇīṁ guṇakathanapuṇyena bhavataḥ
punāmītyarthe'smin puRāmathana buddhirvyavasitā ||3||

3 (a) Meaning and Explanation:

O Brahman! You are the creator of Vedas, the most sublime, musical and nectar like scriptures You are the teacher of great deities like Hiranyagarbha and other divinities. The Goddess of Knowledge and Brihaspati the preceptor of the devatas cannot impress you with their praises and in contrast with such divinities I am a humble human devotee. I submit that my mind is polluted with worldly attachments and I seek to get my mind purified with your grace by my praising your glories.

O Tripuraharā! I am inherently incapable of venturing to praise you. My mind has been inspired by your divine grace and a desire to praise your glories has sprouted in my mind. I venture to proceed with a firm belief that everything happens only by God's will. I am not be blamed for any errors and shortcoming in my praises.

3 (b) The same is applicable in favor of Viṣṇu.

Verse 4

तवैश्वर्यं यत्तज्जगदुदयरक्षाप्रलयकृत्
त्रयीवस्तु व्यस्तं तिसृषु गुणभिन्नासु तनुषु।
अभव्यानामस्मिन् वरद रमणीयामरमणीं
विहन्तुं व्याक्रोशीं विदधत इहैके जडधियः॥ ४॥

tavaiśvaryaṁ yattajjagadudaya rakṣāpralayakṛt
trayīvastu vyastaṁ tisruṣu guṇabhinnāsu tanuṣu |
abhavyānāmasmin Varada Ramaṇīyāmaramaṇīṁ
vihantuṁ vyākrośīṁ vidadhata ihaike jaḍadhiyaḥ || 4 ||

4 (a) Meaning and explanation:

O Varada! meaning the Īśvara who bestows boons. The entire universe including the sky was created by Brahman was envisaged in Vedas. The creation, preservation and destruction in a systematic manner was done by you by dividing the functions respectively between Brahma, Viṣṇu, and Rudra with the three qualities of Tamas, Rajas and Sattva. The reality of which was established with valid Pramānas. However, some illiterate and foolish people who have no idea of their purpose of life who are influenced by atheistic belief deny all this reality. They propagate the falsehood among the people and destabilizes the society.

However, the learned men will not believe and will not be influenced by this false propaganda.

4 (b) The same can be applicable in favor of Viṣṇu.

Verse 5

किमीहः किंकायः स खलु किमुपायस्त्रिभुवनं
किमाधारो धाता सृजति किमुपादान इति च।
अतर्क्यैश्वर्ये त्वय्यनवसर दुःस्थो हतधियः
कुतर्कोऽयं कांश्चित् मुखरयति मोहाय जगतः॥ ५॥

kimīhaḥ kiṁkāyaḥ sa khalu kimupāyastribhuvanaṁ
kimādhāro dhātā sṛjati kimupādāna iti ca |
atarkyaiśvarye tvayyanavasaraduḥstho hatadhiyaḥ
kutarko'yaṁ kāṁścit mukharayati mohāya jagataḥ || 5 ||

5 (a) Meaning and Explanation:

O Parameswara! You are the bestower of all the desires of the devotees. Your auspicious qualities are beyond the scope of any logical discussion. Puṣpadant mentioned the conversation between two dull headed persons.

If a pot has to be manufactured a potter needs mud, a potter's wheel etc. But how can a person without a body create the Universe?. With what purpose and with what instruments and what materials can he create the Universe?. Thus, putting forth dubious illogical, perverted and vociferous propaganda that create delusion among ignorant and gulliable mob. They are called evil.

5 (b) The same is applicable in favor of Viṣṇu.

After refuting the Irrelevant perverted logic by mischievous atheistic arguments, Puṣpadant proceeds to pray mentioning acceptable logic.

Verse 6

अजन्मानो लोकाः किमवयववन्तोऽपि जगतां
अधिष्ठातारं किं भवविधिरनादृत्य भवति।
अनीशो वा कुर्याद् भुवनजनने कः परिकरो
यतो मन्दास्त्वां प्रत्यमरवर संशेरत इमे॥ ६॥

ajanmāno lokāḥ kimavayavavanto'pi jagatāṁ
adhiṣṭhātāraṁ kiṁ bhavavidhiranādṛtya bhavati |
anīśo vā kuryād bhuvanajanane kaḥ parikaro
yato mandāstvāṁ pratyamaravara saṁśerata ime ||6||

6 (a) Meaning and Explanation:

O Mahadeva! You are Parameswara (lord of all and everything) as you are the most superior of all the divinities.

The Bhuloka and all the fourteen worlds are all created, and this was done by a single creator. These worlds are created, sustained, and destroyed. Such a creator has enormous powers unlike a human.

Some atheists with deluded mind argue and try to convince the ignorant mob that it is unbelievable that a person without a body can all alone do all this without any instruments, material.

Puṣpadant refutes all those arguments of evil-minded atheists declared that such a creation is possible to none other than the all-powerful Parameswara and continued his praise of the Lord.

6 (b) The same is applicable in favor of Viṣṇu.

Verse 7

त्रयी साङ्ख्यं योगः पशुपतिमतं वैष्णवमिति
प्रभिन्ने प्रस्थाने परमिदमदः पथ्यमिति च।
रुचीनां वैचित्र्यादृजुकुटिल नानापथजुषां
नृणामेको गम्यस्त्वमसि पयसामर्णव इव॥ ७॥

trayī sāṅkhyaṁ yogaḥ paśupatimataṁ vaiṣṇavamiti
prabhinne prasthāne paramidamadaḥ pathyamiti ca |

rucīnāṁ vaicitryādṛjukuṭila nānāpathajuṣāṁ
nṛṇāmeko gamyastvamasi payasāmarṇava iva || 7 ||

7 (a) Meaning and explanation:

The human beings are very clever. They were born on the earth due to their past deeds. They have desire to get liberated from the bondage.

The Hindu religion has the unique greatness that it has provided different methods for people to choose from the several means of self-realization that suits individual choice according to their ability and attitude. Out of the several means available some choose shorter way or straight path like big rivers Ganga, Godavari etc. flow straight to reach the ocean. Some small rivers such as Yamuna and Sarayu take a zigzag path , join big rivers and take longer time to reach the ocean. But the goal of all is to reach the same destination.

The following are some of the means the Vedas, Samkhya, Patanjali yoga, Vaiṣṇavism, Pasupatham etc., The Nirguna Brahma Upāsakas as prescribed in Vedas are believed to attain Mokṣa quickly. Others who follow other means, even deviating from the teachings of Veda will somehow finally reach Brahman.

Puṣpadant Praises Śiva. Your majesty is too vast and only your devotees can know, and others cannot even imagine. You are an ocean of mercy and refuge for all.

In this connection it is pertinent to mention that Madhusūdana Sarasvati has made a long commentary citing various Vedas, Puranas, Vedāngas, Yoga sastra, Advaita, Vaiṣṇava and several subsects, Sānkhya etc. It was considered as a separate text called Prasthānabheda for some time. As the main topic of this work is Bhakti, the detailed commentary on other means are not discussed here.

Verse 8

महोक्षः खट्वाङ्गं परशुरजिनं भस्म फणिनः
कपालं चेतीयत्तव वरद तन्त्रोपकरणम्।
सुरास्तां तामृद्धिं दधति तु भवद्भूप्रणिहितां
न हि स्वात्मारामं विषयमृगतृष्णा भ्रमयति॥ ८॥

mahokṣaḥ khaṭvāṅgaṁ paraśurajinaṁ Bhasma phaṇinaḥ
kapālaṁ cetīyattava Varada tantropakaraṇam |
surāstāṁ tāmṛddhiṁ dadhati tu bhavadbhūpraṇihitāṁna
hi svātmārāmamaṁ viṣayamṛgatṛṣṇā bhramayati || 8 ||

8 (a) Meaning and Explanation:

O Parameswara! You are the bestower of boons. In your Nirguṇa and Saguṇa Rūpa your glories are infinite. In your Saguṇa swarūpa you appear with seven features. Your attire is a tiger skin, you have an old bull as your vehicle. You have snakes as ornament around your neck, your body is smeared with ash, you have human skull as a bowl, you have an axe and a wooden hand rest (called Khaṭwānga) and Parasu as your weapons held in your hands. Thus, your appearance is that of a poorest of the poor. How can people be inclined to pray such a poor-looking person? However, you grant great boons and wealth to all simply by casting a look. Therefore, your greatness is exceedingly difficult to apprehend. The reason for such a contrast is that you are a great yogi who is free from any worldly attractions and disinterested in pompous paraphernalia. You are the creator of the illusion, but you are free from illusion.

The significance of the items held buy Śiva is as follows. Bull is a symbol of Dharma. It consumes only grass and water, but it gives all its energy to its master. Tiger skin indicates freedom from desire. The ashes indicate the quality of vairagya that all will end in ashes at the end. The serpent has a split tongue and looks fearful. This indicates the ego and hatred and a man must control both these to be at peace. The skull is that of the head of Brahma (the creator) once shredded by Śiva.

8 (b) Explanation as applicable to Viṣṇu:

Viṣṇu reclines on soft and white skin of Great Śeṣanāg floating in the milky ocean (Kṣīrasāgara). The hood of Śeṣanāg is his umbrella. Kaustubha a shining divine jewel is his ornament. He has Sankha (conch shell). An axe and Sudarśan chakra (a powerful discus) are his armaments. He holds a lotus flower in one of his hands. All the demigods and people are blessed with prosperity by the grace of Viṣṇu.

Verse 9

ध्रुवं कश्चित् सर्वं सकलमपरस्त्वध्रुवमिदं
परो ध्रौव्याऽध्रौव्ये जगति गदति व्यस्तविषये।
समस्तेऽप्येतस्मिन् पुरमथन तैर्विस्मित इव
स्तुवन् जिह्रेमि त्वां न खलु ननु धृष्टा मुखरता॥ ९॥

dhruvaṁ kachit sarva sakalamaparastvadhruvamidaṁ
paro dhṛauvyā'dhṛauvye jagati gadati vyasthaviṣaye |
samaste'pyetasmin puRāmathana tairvismita iva
stuvan jihremi tvāṁ na khalu nanu Dṛṣṭa mukharatā ||9 ||

9 (a) Meaning and Explanation:

There are different arguments brought by some people about the creation, existence and dissolution of the world as follows:

One school argues that there is no origin and end to this world. It is everlasting and permanent and Parameswara has no role either in its creation or destruction.

Another sect argue that this world is transitory and it exists one moment and does not exist the other moment and thus it is sūnya (empty or zero or void). Therefore, Īśvara has no role in its creation or dissolution.

A third group of people argue differently from that of the above two groups. They argue that this world is real and not eternal. Some aspects like the all-pervading Sky, earth, atoms etc. are eternal and have no destruction. Some are subjected to destruction. The God may have some role in creation and destruction of the non-permanent aspects but no role in creation of the eternal aspects.

Thus, all the three groups have belief that there is another force other than God, thus the nondual Īśvara has no role.

O Tripuraharā! In view of the above discussion some people feel astonished and hesitate for offering prayers. A man immersed in your devotion will not be aware of being ridiculed but will be intoxicated in his devotional joy. Similarly, I also don't feel ashamed of being ridiculed and offer my prayers to you. Thus, Puṣpadant has expressed his devotion to the Lord.

The above discussion makes it clear that the arguments are not valid and Advaita is real and free from such irrelevant arguments.

9 (b) The same is applicable in favor of Viṣṇu.

Verse 10

तवैश्वर्यं यत्नाद् यदुपरि विरिञ्चिर्हरिरधः
परिच्छेतुं यातावनिलमनलस्कन्धवपुषः।
ततो भक्तिश्रद्धा-भरगुरु-गृणद्भ्यां गिरिश यत्
स्वयं तस्थे ताभ्यां तव किमनुवृत्तिर्न फलति॥ १०॥

tavaiśvaryaṁ yatnād yadupari viriñcirhariradhaḥ
paricchetuṁ yātāvanilamanalaskandhavapuṣaḥ |
tato bhaktiśraddhā-bharaguru-gṛṇadbhyāṁ giriśa yat
svayaṁ tasthe tābhyāṁ tava kimanuvṛttirna phalati ||10||

10 (a) Meaning and explanation:

O Īśvara! You are always in contemplation in Kailas mountain as your abode. Your effulgence brightness is like burning fire, your inconceivably huge form as linga could not be assessed or seen by Brahma and Viṣṇu. They once attempted to find your origin and the top of your liṅga swarūpa. Brahma took the form of a swan and flew to see the head and Viṣṇu took the form of a boar and dug down wards. They got exhausted and gave up and returned. They regretted their action and realized that it is their sheer ego that prompted it. Śiva manifested before them out of compassion. Viṣṇu confessed the truth, but Brahma made a false claim and making 'Ketaki' a flower as a witness. Śiva has punished Brahma for his falsehood by removing one of his five heads and making the Ketaki flower as unfit for worship. Brahma and Viṣṇu have offered whole hearted prayers to Śiva. The benevolent Lord was pleased. Brahma has been delegated the sacred function of creation and Viṣṇu with sustenance and protection of the universe.

The moral is that God showers his grace and blessings on those who shed their ego and pray whole heartedly to the Lord with unconditional love. He will not tolerate deceit or falsehood.

10 (b) Explanation as applicable to Viṣṇu:

The following may be mentioned in Viṣṇu aspect.

"*Girou govardhananakhesete gopīramayannati giriśah sri Viṣṇu*" who reclines on Govardhana mountain surrounded by Gopi's. and can also be stated as *"Girim Mandaramsyati tanukaroti kṣhīroda Madhunniti giriśa*" meaning who has helped in churning of the milky ocean by bearing the mandhar hill. The rest can be same.

Verse 11

अयत्नादासाद्य त्रिभुवनमवैरव्यतिकरं
दशास्यो यद्बाहूनभृत-रणकण्डू-परवशान्|।
शिरःपद्मश्रेणी-रचितचरणाम्भोरुह-बलेः
स्थिरायास्त्वद्भक्तेस्त्रिपुरहर विस्फूर्जितमिदम्||। ११ ||

ayatnādāpādya tribhuvanamavairavyatikaraṁ
daśāsyo yadbāhūnabhṛta-raṇakaṇḍū-paravaśān |
śiraḥpadmaśreṇī-racitacaraṇāmbhoruha-baleḥ
sthirāyā stvadbhaktestripurahara visphūrjitamidam ||11 ||

11 (a) Meaning and explanation:

O Tripuraharā! Rāvaṇa (the demon king) inherently has lot of ego. He was your ardent devotee and at the height of devotion did not hesitate to cut off nine out of his ten heads and offered as lotus flowers at your feet .You were pleased with his devotion and granted him powers.

Rāvaṇa has conquered kingdoms in all the three worlds and annihilated all his enemies. All his powers for achievement of this is due to your grace only.

The benevolent God bestows several boons to his devotees who please him with their sincere devotion.

11 (b) Explanation as applicable in favor of Viṣṇu:

The Lord Viṣṇu out of compassion grants his vision to his devotees. They will be able to cross over the awakening, dreaming state and the deep sleep stages (which are called Tripura) and reach the blissful state called Turīya.

)))

Verse 12

अमुष्य त्वत्सेवा-समधिगतसारं भुजवनं
बलात् कैलासेऽपि त्वदधिवसतौ विक्रमयतः।
अलभ्यापातालेऽप्यलसचलितांगुष्ठशिरसि
प्रतिष्ठा त्वय्यासीद् ध्रुवमुपचितो मुह्यति खलः॥ १२॥

amuṣya tvatsevā-samadhigatasāraṁ bhujavanaṁ
balāt kailāse'pi tvadadhivasatau vikRāmayataḥ |
alabhyāpātāle'pyalasacalitāṁguṣṭhaśirasi
pratiṣṭhā tvayyāsīd dhruvamupacito muhyati khalaḥ ||12 ||

12 (a) Meaning and explanation:

O Īśvara! You are pleased with Rāvaṇa's devotion and granted great powers to him. He was intoxicated with his powers and became so proud that he did not hesitate to pluck the Kailas mountain and take it to his kingdom. Parvati was upset by the shaking of the mountain and prayed to you. You have crushed him with your toe that he shivered with fear and has no space of even an inch of shelter anywhere in the three worlds. Rāvaṇa shivered with fear and humbly begged your forgiveness and you have brought him onto the earth. The moral is that God will not hesitate to punish ungratefulness and ego and nobody can escape punishment for such misdeeds.

12 (b) Explanation as applicable to Viṣṇu:

The emperor Bali was a devotee of Viṣṇu, and he received great wealth and prosperity with the blessing of Viṣṇu. He had performed a yagna for which Viṣṇu attended as a dwarf Brahmin. Bali thought that Vamana is an ordinary Brahmin. Bali has asked Vamana about his desire as a dana. Vamana has replied that he will be pleased with a space of three feet. Bali felt that it is a small desire and accepted it. After getting confirmation from Bali, Vamana occupied the Earth with one foot and sky with another foot and asked Bali where he shall place his foot for the third foot of space offered to him. Bali has humbly bowed down and requested Vamana that he can place his foot on his head. Vamana has then crushed Bali by placing his foot on Bali.

Verse 13

यद्दिं सुत्राम्णो वरद परमोच्चैरपि सतीं
अधश्चक्रे बाणः परिजनविधेयत्रिभुवनः।
न तच्चित्रं तस्मिन् वरिवसितरि त्वच्चरणयोः
न कस्याप्युन्नत्यै भवति शिरसस्त्वय्यवनतिः॥ १३॥

tāmṛddhiṁ sutrāmṇo Varada paramoccairapi satīṁ
adhaścakre bāṇaḥ parijanavidheyatribhuvanaḥ |
na taccitraṁ tasmin varivaSītari tvaccaraṇayoḥ
na kasyāpyunnatyai bhavati śirasastvayyavanatiḥ || 13 ||

13 (a) Meaning and Explanation:

O Varada! You bestow boons to devotees and fulfill all their desires. Bānāsura (the demon king) is your great devotee. You were pleased with his devotion and you have granted him immense wealth and powers that he has accrued wealth to the extent that he exceeded Indra (the king of heaven) in wealth. This is not surprising as you will bless all irrespective of whether he is a demigod, demon, or a human, who have sincere and unwavering devotion to you.

13 (b) Explanation as applicable to Viṣṇu:

The following explanation can be mentioned.

The word (Bāna) means arrow. The word Sutramna+bāna means the arrow of Indra, the king of heaven. The combination of *Utchaih + api. adhah + api. satimbudhim)* means wealth spread in three worlds, *chakre* = gets. Indra could accrue such great wealth is not surprising as he has prostrated with his head at the lotus feet of Viṣṇu. He has acquired the ability to win over all the demons with one arrow. Anybody who has ardent devotion to Viṣṇu would be brought to the height of glory.

Verse 14

अकाण्ड-ब्रह्माण्ड-क्षयचकित-देवासुरकृपा
विधेयस्याऽऽसीद्‌ यस्त्रिनयन विषं संहृतवतः।
स कल्माषः कण्ठे तव न कुरुते न श्रियमहो
विकारोऽपि श्लाघ्यो भुवन-भय- भङ्ग- व्यसनिनः॥ १४॥

akāṇḍa-brahmāṇḍa-kṣayacakita-devāsurakṛpā
vidheyasyā''sīd yastrinayana viṣaṁ saṁhṛtavataḥ |
sa kalmāṣaḥ kaṇṭhe tava na kurute na śriyamaho
vikāro'pi ślāghyo bhuvana-bhaya- bhaṅga- vyasaninaḥ
|| 14 ||

14 (a) Meaning and explanation:

O Trinayana! You have Sun, moon, and fire as your three eyes. You are compassionate to all. When deities and demons are churning the milky ocean a fountain of deadly poison called *Kālakūta* that can burn all the three worlds has come up. All were frightened. They have all including Viṣṇu and Brahma have approached you seeking protection. You out of compassion have swallowed the poison and held it in your throat which turned black and a black stain remained. This is considered auspicious and people worship and address you as Nīlakhanta. The stain is praiseworthy and believed to dispel all fears.

14 (b) Explanation applicable to Viṣṇu:

There was a great deluge, and the entire world was inundated with water. The demigods and demons approached Viṣṇu to save the world. He generously agreed and as an incarnation ***Vāraha*** (the great wild boar) dried all the water.

As he came out of the slush a bluish black layer remained on the body. The praise of the beauty of the Lord fills the throats of the devotees with auspiciousness.

Verse 15

असिद्धार्था नैव क्वचिदपि सदेवासुरनरे
निवर्तन्ते नित्यं जगति जयिनो यस्य विशिखाः।
स पश्यन्नीश त्वामितरसुरसाधारणमभूत्
स्मरः स्मर्तव्यात्मा न हि वशिषु पथ्यः परिभवः॥ १५॥

asiddhārthā naiva kvacidapi sadevāsuranare
nivartante nityaṁ jagati jayino yasya viśikhāḥ |
sa paśyannīśa tvāmitarasurasādhāraṇamabhūt
smaraḥ smartavyātmā na hi vaśiṣu pathyaḥ paribhavaḥ ||15||

15 (a) Meaning and Explanation:

Sankara! The god of love Manmadha has a record that his flower decked arrow has never failed in all the three worlds. He thought that you are also like any other deity and dared to attempt to shoot his arrow on you. When you glanced him with your third eye he was burnt like a piece of straw and remained formless. You are the supreme yogi and his audacity caused him the damage. Thus Puṣpadanta praised Siva's glory that He is *Jetendriya* (one who conquers his own sensory organs). Those who intend to harm Īśvara will face miseries in their lives.

15 (b) Explanation applicable to Viṣṇu:

As per Puranic story Manmadha has taken birth seeing

Viṣṇu, they exchanged glances. The legend is that father sees the newborn son and the baby also sees his father for the first time. The son usually inherits the qualities of his parent as per scriptural saying *'Ātmavyai putranāmasi'*. According to this analogy Manmadha and Viṣṇu have such relationship. But they have opposite nature. Viṣṇu has the nature of getting the people out of mundane desires and take them towards self-realization, whereas Manmadha tries to win over people and entice them to passion and desires. The rest of the glories can be described as above.

Verse 16

महीपादाघाताद् व्रजति सहसा संशयपदं
पदं विष्णोर्भ्राम्यद् भुज-परिघ-रुग्ण-ग्रह- गणम्।
मुहुर्द्यौर्दौस्थ्यं यात्यनिभृत-जटा-ताडित-तटा
जगद्रक्षायै त्वं नटसि ननु वामैव विभुता॥ १६॥

mahīpādāghātād vrajati sahasā saṁśayapadaṁ
padaṁ Viṣṇoh bhrāmyad bhuja-parigha-rugṇa-graha-gaṇam |
muhurdyauṛdausthyaṁ yātyanibhṛta-jaṭā-tāḍita-taṭā
jagadrakṣāyai tvāṁ naṭasi nanu vāmaiva vibhutā || 16 ||

16 (a) Meaning and Explanation:

O Śiva! You perform *Tāndava nṛitya* every day at *Pradoṣakāla* (at dusk time) for the welfare of the people. The tread of your feet make it feel that the earth will be broken to pieces and the stars and planets may fall due to hard strokes of your strong and huge shoulders hitting the heaven, the hard strokes of your matted plaits of hair on the borders of Indra's kingdom causes suffering. It is strange that although the purpose of the dance is for welfare, the inhabitants of the worlds are subjected to fear and suffering for a short time. It is like taking a bitter medicine to cure a serious disease.

The Purāṇic story goes like this: A demon has made a severe penance to Brahma. Brahma was pleased and asked him to choose a boon. The demon asked that all the worlds should be subjected to suffering every day at the time of dusk and seeing their suffering is his delight. Brahma agreed but held it for some time. All deities approached Śiva to protect them. Śiva without waging any war with the demon, thought of a novel plan. He decided to dance every day at dusk. Brahma, Viṣṇu, Sarasvati, and other deities participated in the dance by playing musical instruments and praying at that time. The demon was also witnessing the dance and fully immersed in enjoying the spectacular dance and forgot his desired boon. Thus, the sufferings of the worlds have been averted.

16 (b) Explanation applicable to Viṣṇu:

When dharma has been broken down, unruly behavior will reign in the world. The non-believers of God will violate all principals and do not hesitate to spoil the spiritual rituals and sacred places of worship. Even priests will become atheists. The masses will be intoxicated by drinking liquor and dominated by demonic thoughts.

In such a situation the Lord will incarnate to punish the evil and protect the pious people and reestablish the dharma in the world.

Verse 17

विय-द्व्या पी तारा-गण-गुणित-फेनोद्गम-रुचिः
प्रवाहो वारां यः पृषतलघुदृष्टः शिरसि ते।
जगद्द्वीपाकारं जलधिवलयं तेन कृतमिति
अनेनैवोन्नेयं धृतमहिम दिव्यं तव वपुः॥ १७॥

viya-dvyā pī tārā-gaṇa-guṇita-phenodgama-ruci
pravāho vārāṁ yaḥ pṛṣatalaghudṛṣṭaḥ śirasi te |
jagaddvīpākāraṁ jaladhivalayaṁ tena kṛtamiti
anenaivonneyaṁ dhṛtamahima divyaṁ tava vapuḥ ||17||

17 (a) Meaning and Explanation:

O Parameswara! The effulgence of the river flowing over your hair is reflected and looks like tiny flakes of foam, exceedingly brighter than the stars in the sky. This is Ākāsaganga brought down by sage Bhagīratha from heaven. The mighty river looks like a drop of water on your head and from this your magnificence is beyond comprehension.

Once sage Agastya had swallowed all the water on the earth including oceans. After some time, sage Bhagīratha meditated and pleased Viṣṇu to let the celestial river Mandākinī to be sent on to the earth. The thrust of the fall of the river cannot be faced by the earth. At the request of all, Śiva agreed that the river may fall from heaven on his head and then will slide down from his matted plaits. The river looked like a drop of water on Śiva's head and the flow of water has filled all the oceans. Therefore, the size of the body of Śiva and his magnificence can be considered beyond imagination. Brahman is all pervading and the whole world is contained in Him.

The river is called Mandākinī in heaven. It is called Bhagīrathi or Ganga on land and as Bhogāvathi in Pātalaloka.

17 (b): Explanation as applicable to Viṣṇu:

Viṣṇu while attending the yagna of Bali has taken incarnation as Vāmana. When Vāmana has placed his foot on the head of Bali for completing the third foot of space offered by Bali crushed him with his toe. The thrust has driven Bali to Pātalaloka that shacked the Brahmaloka, (the topmost loka) and the river flowing from the cosmic egg. This looked like a droplet before Viṣṇu. Thus, Viṣṇu's magnificence is beyond imagination of any body. The rest of the explanation as mentioned for Śiva.

Verse 18

रथः क्षोणी यन्ता शतधृतिरगेन्द्रो धनुरथो
रथाङ्गे चन्द्रार्कौ रथ-चरण-पाणिः शर इति।
दिधक्षोस्त्ते कोऽयं त्रिपुरतृणमाडम्बर विधिः
विधेयैः क्रीडन्त्यो न खलु परतन्त्राः प्रभुधियः॥ १८॥

radhaḥ kṣoṇī yantā śatadhṛtiragendro dhanuratho
rathāṅge candrārkau ratha-caraṇa-pāṇiḥ śara iti |
didhakṣoste ko'yaṁ tripuratṛṇamāḍambara vidhiḥ
vidheyaiḥ krīḍantyo na khalu paratantrāḥ prabhudhiyaḥ ||18||

18 (a) Meaning and explanation:

O Parameswara!

There was a demon called Tripurāsura who has three sons named Vidyunmāli, Tārakāsura and Kamalāsksudu. They have three cities with gold, silver, and iron chariots over which they roam about. They have a boon from Brahma (the creator) that they will not have normal death. They can be killed only by one arrow all at the same time. They meet only once in thousand years. So, it is not possible for any ordinary person to kill them. The demigods were vexed with the troubles created by them. They approached Śiva and prayed to put an end to their troubles. Śiva agreed that he will help only when they arrange support by providing suitable chariot and all armaments for war.

They have arranged the earth as a chariot, the Sun and moon as its wheels. and Brahma as charioteer. The Meru mountain as a bow and Viṣṇu as an arrow. Thus, organized a paraphernalia to kill Tripurasuras. When once Tripurasuras assembled met on the bank of Narmada River, Siva killed them with one arrow. Siva has the power to burn all the three worlds like a piece of straw in a wink by mere will. All this was done as a sport. It is only to show His command over all demigods.

18 (b) Explanation as applicable to Viṣṇu:

The word Tripura can be understood as the city built on Trikutagiri (Island city) for Rāvaṇa. When Rāvaṇa kidnapped Sitādevi (the consort of Rāma), and kept her captive in his island city. Rāma could found out her location after a strenuous search with the help of Sugrīva (the monkey king).

Rāma decided to wage a war on Rāvaṇa and consulted Sugriva, Laxman, Vibhīṣaṇa (brother of Rāvaṇa who sought asylum of Rāma), Hanuman and others. He has mobilized an army of monkeys and constructed a bridge between the mainland and the Island with the help of the monkeys (monkeys are always fickle minded). He has arranged a chariot and necessary armaments for the war and finally killed Rāvaṇa. Rāma being an incarnation could have annihilated Rāvaṇa like a piece of straw in a wink by mere decision and all this Paraphernalia was not at all necessary. It is only to show as if he were a human. It is only an act of sport.

Verse 19

हरिस्ते साहस्रं कमल बलिमाधाय पदयोः
यदेकोने तस्मिन् निजमुदहरन्नेत्रकमलम्।
गतो भक्त्युद्रेकः परिणतिमसौ चक्रवपुषः
त्रयाणां रक्षायै त्रिपुरहर जागर्ति जगताम्॥ १९॥

hariste sāhasraṁ kamala balimādhāya padayoḥ
radhyekone tasmin nijamudahāra netrakamalam |
gato bhaktoudrekaḥ pariṇatimasau cakravapuṣaḥ
trayāṇāṁ rakṣāyai tripurahara jāgarti jagatām || 19 ||

19 (a) Meaning and Explanation.:

O Śaṅkara!

Śrī MahāViṣṇu is your devotee and wished to worship your lotus feet with one thousand lotus flowers and arranged all required items and started the worship. You were deeply impressed with his devotion, but to test him you removed one lotus and hid it. Viṣṇu found that one flower was missing. He intended to remove one of his eyes and offer at your feet so that the vow may not become futile. When he removed his own eye, you have appeared before him and placed the eye back in its place. You were pleased with his ardent devotion and blessed Viṣṇu and gave him the charge of sustenance of the three worlds and the great 'Sudarśan' discus as an instrument that will be useful in the protection of the worlds. This is a proof of your grace and love towards your devotees and generous blessings beyond the expectation of your devotees.

19 (b) Explanation applicable to Viṣṇu:

The name Hari has a meaning as Indra. Indra (a demigod), is a devotee of Viṣṇu. He has one thousand eyes on his body which look like lotus flowers, He worshipped Viṣṇu with one thousand lotus flowers and had darśan with his one thousand eyes. Viṣṇu was pleased with the concentration and single minded devotion of Indra and granted him a boon to be the king of heaven which has all riches: very precious things like the unique white elephant called Irāvatam, the wish fulling tree called 'Kalpataru', the sacred cow called Kāmadhenu, the magical horse called 'Uchchaihshravas' and the nectar called Amrut which gives immortality. This is the proof of the grace and benevolence of Viṣṇu who bestows blessing beyond the expectation of the devotee.

Verse 20

क्रतौ सुप्ते जाग्रत्‌ त्वमसि फलयोगे क्रतुमतां
क्व कर्म प्रध्वस्तं फलति पुरुषाराधनमृते।
अतस्त्वां सम्प्रेक्ष्य क्रतुषु फलदान-प्रतिभुवं
श्रुतौ श्रद्धां बध्वा दृढपरिकरः कर्मसु जनः॥ २०॥

kratau supte jāgrattvamasi phalayoge kratumatāṁ
kva karma pradhvastaṁ phalati puruṣārādhanāmṛte |
atastvāṁ saṁprekṣya kratuṣu phaladāna-pratibhuvaṁ
śrutau śraddhāṁ badhvā kṛthaparikaraḥ karmasu janaḥ
|| 20 ||

20 (a) Meaning and Explanation:

O Parameswara!

You are the bestower of the appropriate fruits of the fire sacrifices and rituals performed as prescribed in the scriptures. Such rituals should be performed with dedication and sincere devotion and faith in God. Then only they are eligible for appropriate fruits of the actions. You are awake and ready to bestow the appropriate fruits when the ritual is completed.

However, some perverted people perform such rituals in a mechanical manner without any devotion towards the Lord. So, such persons do not get the fruits of such actions.

Therefore, everyone should realize that without the grace of the Lord, rituals performed will not give any fruits and devotion to the Lord is essential.

20 (b) Explanation as applicable to Viṣṇu:

The same explanation can be said as applicable in favour of Viṣṇu.

The last sentence "*śrutau śraddhāṁ badhvā kṛthapari-karaḥ karmasu janaḥ*" has the meaning as follows. A person of sublime character, who performs the rituals as prescribed in the scriptures gives delight to all, being nonviolent and with full of compassion to all. Therefore, it can be construed that rituals performed as prescribed in the scriptures with full faith and devotion to the Lord will surely bear fruit.

Verse 21

क्रियादक्षो दक्षः क्रतुपतिरधीशस्तनुभृतां
ऋषीणामार्त्विज्यं शरणद सदस्याः सुर-गणाः।
क्रतुभ्रंशस्त्वत्तः क्रतुफल-विधान-व्यसनिनः
ध्रुवं कर्तुं श्रद्धा विधुरमभिचाराय हि मखाः॥ २१॥

kriyādakṣo dakṣaḥ kratupatiradhīśa stanubhṛtāṁ
mṛṣīṇāmātrivijyam śaraṇada sadasyāḥ sura-gaṇāḥ |
kratubhraṁśastvattaḥ kratuphala-vidhāna-vyasaninaḥ
dhruvaṁ katruṁ Śraddhā vidhuRāmabhicārāya hi makhāḥ
|| 21 ||

21 (a) Meaning and Explanation:

O Parama Śiva! Dakṣa who is called Prajāpati is, the Lord of all people. He has thorough knowledge of all the scriptur-al practices and has decided to perform a Yagna. He has the great sage Bhṛugu and several proficient in Vedas as advisers and conductors of the ritual proceedings. He has invited all the deities including Brahma, Viṣṇu, Indra and others. He has intentionally avoided inviting Śiva, the principal deity to be propitiated at yagna, and Pārvati who is the consort of Śiva (also his own daughter) due to his hatred towards Śiva. Despite that, out love for her father Pārvati arrived at the function but, she was humiliated by her father as also by the family as per her father's instructions. Pārvathi could not tolerate the humiliation and burnt herself with her divine powers. Śiva became furious on Dakṣa and deputed his son to destruct the yagna.

The performance of yagna and seeking fruits thereof but without the due dedication and faith will not only be ending in devastation but also cause misfortune to the performer. Dakṣa is himself the cause for the destruction of his Yagna. He lost his mental balance due to hatred on Śiva and unaware that Śiva is the supreme deity.

21 (b) Explanation as applicable to Viṣṇu:

The explanation can be given as follows. If "*kriyādakṣo dakṣaḥ*" is split as *Kriyādakṣa+uddaksaḥ* which means, who is well versed and competent in performing the yagna and having well-built Physique. The meaning of the words "*adhīśa stanubhṛtāṁ*" may be interpreted as 'tanubhṛtāṁ' meaning who has the nature of only nursing his body which can be interpreted as a demon or of huge body. and "*adhīśa*" the powerful. Thus, it is inferred as the demon emperor Bali. Bali was a devotee of Viṣṇu and performed a yagna and invited all deities, He has intentionally not invited Indra the king of heaven and a devotee of Viṣṇu.

Viṣṇu felt that insult to his devotee as an insult to himself, however attended the yagna as a dwarf brahmin youth called Vāmana (It is an incarnation of the Viṣṇu). Bali is not aware of this and considered him as any other Brahmin. He offered a dāna and Vāmana has asked for three feet of land. After getting reassurance from Bali that he will abide by the offer, he accepted. Viṣṇu has occupied the earth by placing one of his foot, the entire sky with the second foot and asked where he will get the space for placing his third foot. Bali has bowed before Vāmana and offered his head to place the foot of Vāmana to fulfill his promise. Viṣṇu placed his foot on Bali's head and crushed Bali into Pātalaloka. Thus, Viṣṇu punished Bali for the insult to His devotee Indra.

Verse 22

प्रजानाथं नाथ प्रसभमभिकं स्वां दुहितरं
गतं रोहिद् भूतां रिरमयिषुमृष्यस्य वपुषा।
धनुष्पाणेर्यातं दिवमपि सपत्राकृतममुं
त्रसन्तं तेऽद्यापि त्यजति न मृगव्याधरभसः॥ २२॥

prajānāthaṁ nātha prasabhamabhikaṁ svāṁ duhitaraṁ
gataṁ rohid bhūtam rirāmayiṣumṛṣyasya vapuṣā |
dhanuṣpāṇeryātaṁ divamapi sapatrākṛtamamuṁ
trasantaṁ te'dyāpi tyajati na mṛgavyādharabhasaḥ || 22 ||

22 (a) Meaning and Explanation:

There is a puranic story as follows.:

Brahma is the creator of the universe and maintainer of the Dharma. During the process of creation, he has created a feminine person called Sandhya (also called Sarasvati). she has enchanting beauty. He was enamored of her. He has advanced towards her seeking a romantic union unmindful of presence of his sons. She was ashamed and with repulsion ran away taking the form of a feminine deer (called Rohini). Brahma followed her taking the form of a male deer. Śiva who happened to see this got furious for the unethical behavior of Brahma. Śiva took his bow and shot an arrow aimed at Brahma. Brahma then flew to the sky. In the galaxy of stars, we find the star Rohini followed by Mrigasira and Ārudra behind Mrigasira. Rohini is identified as Sarasvati and Mrigasira as Brahma following them is Ārudra as Śiva's arrow chasing Brahma. Thus, Śiva's arrow is implied as is still chasing Brahma to discipline him.

Brahma is endowed with complete knowledge of the Vedas. Sarasvati (the goddess of learning and arts) is Sabda rūpa meaning voice. It is well known that knowledge cannot be understood without voice. Thus, they are indivisible. The secret meaning of Brahma desiring union with her is to be understood as that they cannot exist in separation.

It was mentioned by Poet Kālidās in the Mangalācarana sloka in his composition 'Harivamsa';

'*Vagardhā vivasaṁprokttou Vagārdhā pratipattaye*
Jagatahpitarou vande Pārvatīparameśwaraoh"

Meaning just as voice and meaning are inseparable so also Pārvati and Parameśwara are always together.

22 (b) Explanation applicable to Viṣṇu:

In Rāmāyanā, there was a mischievous demon named Māricha who used to subject human beings and sages to troubles. He has embarked on a plan to help Rāvaṇa kidnap Sīta from their hermitage. He will take the form of a beautiful deer and attract the attention of Sīta who will tell Rāma that she is fond of the deer and asks Rāma to fetch it for her. When Rāma tries to catch the deer, it will run and take Rāma far away. When Rāma is nearing the deer, it will loudly shout the name of Lakṣmana in the tone of Rāma. Then Lakṣmana apprehending some trouble for his brother will run for rescuing him. Sīta will thus be left alone without guard and Rāvaṇa can come in disguise of a Riṣi and could easily kidnap Sīta. The plan was well executed and when Rāma identified that it is not a real deer but a demon who took the form of the deer shot an arrow on Māricha and killed him. Before dying Māricha shouted the name of Lakṣmana in the tone of Rāma. Sīta who heard the voice of Rāma persuaded Lakṣmana to rush to save Rāma in danger. He does not want Sita to be left alone but, due to persistence of Sīta left the Āśrama towards Rāma.

Rāvaṇa then kidnapped Sīta. Thus, the episode of Rāma (an incarnation of Viṣṇu) killing the demon Māricha in disguise of a deer is popular.

Verse 23

स्वलावण्याशंसा धृतधनुषमह्नाय तृणवत्
पुरः प्लुष्टं दृष्ट्वा पुरमथन पुष्पायुधमपि।
यदि स्त्रैणं देवी यमनिरत-देहार्ध-घटनात्
अवैति त्वामद्धा बत वरद मुग्धा युवतयः॥ २३॥

svalāvaṇyāśaṁsā dhṛtadhanuṣamahnyāya tṛṇavat
puraḥ pluṣṭaṁ dṛṣṭvā puramathana puṣpāyudhamapi |
yadi straiṇaṁ devī yamanirata-dehārdha-ghaṭanāt
davaiti tvāmaddhā bata Varada Mugdha yuvatayaḥ || 23 ||

23 (a) Meaning and Explanation:

O Tripura hara!

You are the Parama yogi. You have opened your third eye and the Love God Manmadha was burnt like a piece of straw in the presence of your consort Pārvati who is a rigorous follower of yoga and a disciplined beautiful lady. You have shared half of self with her having been pleased with her penance and became Ardhanāreśwara, but she thought that you did it due to fascination for her beauty. It is due to her feminine nature which is ignorance or lack of proper understanding. Although she is divine, in Saguṇa rūpa she considers herself the daughter of Himavanta.

The puranic story is as follows: Śiva's consort is Pārvati the daughter of the Himalayan king. He also bears River Ganga on his head and therefore, Ganga is also considered as his second consort. Pārvathi is a beautiful lady.

She practices the yoga following the Yama, Niyama and other prescribed practices. She made rigorous penance as daughter of Himavanta and got married to Śiva. One day she closed the eyes of Śiva from behind as a sport. Then all the worlds were filled with pitch darkness and all were perturbed. Śiva hurriedly opened his third eye and fire broke out and mountains and forests started burning. Pārvathi observed the unusual happenings and removed her hands. Śiva has reprimanded her and narrated that though it is a minute period for her, several yugas have lapsed on earth. She repented for her childish action and made a severe penance at Kāncipuram. Parameśwara was incredibly pleased with her devotion and at her promise (not to recur such earlier incidence) shared half of his self with Pārvati and became Ardhanāreśwara. Yet, due to her inherent feminine human nature she feels that Śiva gave her half body as he was fascinated by her beauty. It is because that she still did not forgot that she was a daughter of Himavanta.

23 (b) Explanation as applicable to Viṣṇu:

In the line three of the verse *"Ardhaghatana Daśa"* can be understood as "O Viṣṇu! who In the incarnation as Rāma has been in close association with Sīta who is incarnation of Laxmi, with no scope of separation." Sīta is '*Yamaniratadeha*h' meaning a very pious loyal lady. '*Purāmadhanapuṣpa*' means having delicate and an incredibly soft skin that cannot tolerate even a touch by a flower.

The word 'Svalāvaṇyāśaṁsā' can be understood as who is proud of own valor etc.

Rāma for protection of Sīta, '*Dhrutadhanusham*' has borne the bow and arrows. The word *"Ahnāya trunvatpurah pluṣ-*

tam" means who have burnt the Island city like a piece of straw. Despite being aware of all the qualities of Rāma (a divine inherently) she thought that all these deeds were done by Rāma because of fascination for her. It must be construed as, nothing but her inherent ignorance.

Verse 24

श्मशानेष्वाक्रीडा स्मरहर पिशाचाः सहचराः
चिता-भस्मालेपः स्रगपि नृकरोटी-परिकरः।
अमङ्गल्यं शीलं तव भवतु नामैवमखिलं
तथापि स्मर्तृणां वरद परमं मङ्गलमसि॥ २४॥

śmaśāneṣvākrīḍā smarahara piśācāḥ sahacarāḥ
citā-bhasmālepaḥ sragapi nṛkaroṭī-parikaraḥ |
amaṅgalyaṁ śīlaṁ tava bhavatu nāmaivamakhilaṁ
tathāpi smartṝṇāṁ varada parāmaṁ maṅgalamasi || 24 ||

24 (a) Meaning and Explanation:

O Varada!

It is not possible for anybody to imagine your magnificence by your appearance. You are always seen playing blissfully among the ghosts in the graveyard. your body is smeared with the ashes from the funeral piers, you have the tiger skin as your attire, you have fearful snakes as your ornament around your neck, you have a garland of human skulls and all these are seemingly inauspicious. However, you give boons to all those who worship you with devotion and ensure welfare to them.

The devotion has two objectives (i) for fulfillment of desires and benefits to be enjoyed in the mundane world (Ihiham) (ii) The second is for attainment of Mokṣa (Āmuṣmika) or other worldly aspiration.

Śiva has revealed the reasons for making the burial ground as his sporting ground etc. He said that the evil forces around him are under control and if he roams around, they will also follow and they may intimidate and cause trouble to the people. The burial ground is the last place for humans, and it is conducive to attain mokṣa. I will be helping them. The snakes, and ashes etc. are all my characteristic features. The whole world is '*Agnisomatmakam*' meaning that the is full of burning mass as well as cool, of which I represent the fire aspect and Viṣṇu the Soma aspect. I assure and grant fruits desired to those who worship me knowing my auspiciousness and not the external appearance.

24 (b) Explanation applicable to Viṣṇu:

The words in the sloka can be arranged as " *Tava smaranam amangalayam bhavatunama tadhapitesham*"

Tvameva sarvamangala: Meaning that, even if the character of those worship you is inauspicious, you will bestow them with all auspiciousness. The same is mentioned in Bhagavat-Gita (9.30)

Verse 25

मनः प्रत्यक् चित्ते सविधमविधायात्त-मरुतः
प्रहृष्यद्रोमाणः प्रमद-सलिलोत्सङ्गति-दृशः।
यदालोक्याह्लादं ह्रद इव निमज्यामृतमये
दधत्यन्तस्तत्त्वं किमपि यमिनस्तत् किल भवान्॥ २५॥

manaḥ pratyak citte savidhamavidhāyātta-marutaḥ
prahṛṣyadromāṇaḥ pramada-salilotsaṅgati-dṛśaḥ |
yadālokyāhlādaṁ hrada iva nimajyāmṛtamaye
dadhatyantastattvaṁ kimapi yaminastat kila bhavān ||25 ||

25 (a) Meaning and Explanation:

O Īśvara!

The yogis who practice the prescribed yogic regulations like Yama, Niyama, Āsana, Prānayama, Pratyāhara, Dhārana, Dhyāna, the eight-fold yoga and attain Samādhi state. Prior to that they control the manas which one of the four aspects of their inner organ (Citta, Ahaṁkāra or Ego, Buddhi and Manas).and merge it with citta. Then they visualize the self-effulugent and ever blissful Brahman. They will be overwhelmed with joy and their eyes filled with tears of joy; their bodies experience divinely created goosebumps. They feel that they are bathing in lake of nectar. The reason behind all this is the aspect of the supreme God head.

The stanza thus poetically describes Nirguṇa tattva, the one without second which is ever blissful effulgence and mass of truth which is called Brahman.

25 (b) The explanation as applicable to Viṣṇu: The same is applicable for Viṣṇu.

Verse 26

त्वमर्कस्त्वं सोमस्त्वमसि पवनस्त्वं हुतवहः
त्वमापस्त्वं व्योम त्वमु धरणिरात्मा त्वमिति च।
परिच्छिन्नामेवं त्वयि परिणता बिभ्रति गिरं
न विद्मस्तत्तत्त्वं वयमिह तु यत्‌ त्वं न भवसि॥ २६॥

tvamarkastvaṁ somastvamasi pavanastvaṁ hutavahaḥ
tvamāpastvaṁ vyoma tvamu dharaṇi rātmātvamitica |
paricchinnāmevaṁ tvayi pariṇatā bibhratu giraṁ
na vidmastattattvaṁ vayamihatu yattvaṁ na bhavasi ||26||

26 (a) Meaning and Explanation:

O Parameswara!

You are the all-pervading, omnipresent, supreme, without limits. However, some people who have not acquired the correct knowledge about your glory describe you as a finite entity like Earth, Sun, Moon, wind, fire, water, sky, and soul. There is a legend of eight forms of Rudra as follows called asṭa murtis'. By adding namaḥ to it they become eight mantras for worshipping Śiva. These mantras should be learnt from a qualified guru. These are the names of the different forms of the Lord.

i) Bhava - Existence, Creation (ii) Sharva - Destroyer (of darkness and evil) iii) Rudra - Dispeller of sorrows. iv) Pasupathi - Lord of all beings. (v) Ugra - The fearsome (vi) Mahan: the supreme. (vii) Bhima - The tremendous and (viii) Īsana - The directional ruler.

However, we are not aware of any object which is not containing you and anything in which you are not present, meaning that the Lord is all pervading and omnipresent. Thus Puṣpadanta emphasizes the nondual aspect of the Lord.

26 (b) Explanation applicable to Viṣṇu:

Nārāyana also pervades all over and omnipresent. The name Sūrya (Sun) is also popular as Sūryanārāyana. It is mentioned in Bṛahadāraṇyaka Upaniṣad as follows. "*Yayeva asso ādittyecpuruṣah Yeta deva aham brahma upāsye*". The rest is same.

Verse 27

त्रयीं तिस्रो वृत्तीस्त्रिभुवनमथो त्रीनपि सुरान्
अकाराद्यैर्वर्णैस्त्रिभिरभिदधत् तीर्णविकृति।
तुरीयं ते धाम ध्वनिभिरवरुन्धानमणुभिः
समस्त-व्यस्तं त्वां शरणद गृणात्योमिति पदम्॥ २७॥

trayīṁ tisro vṛttīstribhuvanamatho trīnapi surān
nakārādyairvarṇaistribhirabhidadhat tīrṇavikṛti |
turīyaṁ te dhāma dhvanibhiravarundhāna maṇubhiḥ
samasta-vyastaṁ tvāṁ śaraṇada gṛṇātyomiti padaṁ || 27||

27 (a) Meaning and Explanation:

O Mahadeva!

You are the protector of the entire universe. The word OM is a composite and formed by a combination of three alphabets Aa, Vu, Ma and half alphabet. The composite word is used to address your name. It connotes three Vedas (Rig, Yajur and Sāma), three states (awakening, dream and deep sleep) and also creation, being and dissolution The sound also include Brahma, Viṣṇu and Śiva. The three lokas Heaven, earth and Pāthāla.

The composite word OM is called "Brahma Praṇava" indicates your advaitic oneness and the Turīya state. The individual alphabets denote your Saguṇa aspects.

27 (b) The same is applicable in respect of Viṣṇu.

Verse 28

भवः शर्वो रुद्रः पशुपतिरथोग्रः सहमहान्
तथा भीमेशानाविति यदभिधानाष्टकमिदम्।
अमुष्मिन् प्रत्येकं प्रविचरति देव श्रुतिरपि
प्रियायास्मैधाम्ने प्रणिहित-नमस्योऽस्मि भवते॥ २८॥

bhavaḥ śarvo rudraḥ paśupatirathograḥ sahamahān
sthathā bhīmeśānāviti yadabhidhānāṣṭakamidam |
amuṣmin pratyekaṁ pravicarati deva śrutirapi
priyāyāsmaidhāmne praṇihita-namasyo'smi bhavate
||28||

28 (a) Meaning and Explanation:

Puṣpadanta in the earlier stanza described the significance of the Brahma Praṇava OM and it was specified to address the Nirguṇa aspect of the Lord. Now he discusses the eight different names as mentioned in Vedas as names for the manifest form of the Lord.

O Mahadeva! The Vedas only are competent authority to describe your different names and their significance. There are eight such names whose significance was described, and they are also called Mantras. Whosoever praise the Lord with these names will be blessed by the Lord and they achieve their goals easily.

The Last stanza above *"priyāyāsmaidhāmne praṇihita-namasyo'smi"* means The devotee prays to the lord for reaching the place which is dear to you (The Kailās mountain is most cherished place of Śiva). The eight names have been mentioned in Viṣṇu purāṇa eighth adhyaya. Each of the eight names indicate different powers of the Lord. The-Lord has at the time of creation of the world has taken different roles. They are water, earth, sun, Fire, Yagnadeekshita, moon, sky, wind, these eight aspects have eight names and they are the names of asṭarudrās and are used for praying Śiva.

i) *Bhavāya Kṣitimurtayenamah. (ii) Sarvāya Jalamū tayenamah. (iii) Ugrāya Tejomūrthayenamah 1v) Bhemaya kasamūrthayenamah. (v) Mahādevay Somamūrthayenamah. (vi) Pasupathaye - yagnamūrthayenamah. (vii) Iśāna arkamūrthayenamah. (viii) Ruraya vayumūrthayenamah.*

O Lord! Whatever different names you may have, the most loving feature is your swarūpa. It has greatness which is not possible to be described exhaustively and I prostrate and bow down and offer my aṣṭānga panama(eight limbed prostration).

28 (b) Explanation applicable in favor of Viṣṇu:

It is explained that if we add "Deva" to each of the above names of Śiva like Bhava deva, Sarva deva, Ugradeva etc. they will be equally applicable to Viṣṇu.

The names like Bhava are available in Viṣṇu Sahasranāma stotra and all the names are equally applicable to Śiva and Viṣṇu.

Verse 29

नमो नेदिष्ठाय प्रियदव दविष्ठाय च नमः
नमः क्षोदिष्ठाय स्मरहर महिष्ठाय च नमः।
नमो वर्षिष्ठाय त्रिनयन यविष्ठाय च नमः
नमः सर्वस्मै ते तदिदमतिसर्वाय च नमः॥ २९॥

namo nediṣṭhāya priyadava daviṣṭhāya ca namaḥ namo
kṣodiṣṭhāya smarahara mahiṣṭhāya ca namaḥ |
namo varṣiṣṭhāya trinayana yaviṣṭhāya ca namo namaḥ
sarvasmai te tadidamati sarvāya ca namaḥ || 29 ||

29 (a) Meaning and Explanation:

Puṣpadanta starts his prayer as

O Īśvara! You are in the proximity and extremely far away, you are tiniest and mightiest, you are youthful and aged, you have all forms and are also formless. You have such mutually opposite qualities and you are all pervading. It is exceedingly difficult to comprehend your qualities for ordinary people. I again and again offer my Namaskāras to you and beg your pardon.

i) Salutations to the Lord who is very close (to his devotees) and He is far away (from those not devoted)

ii) Salutations to Smarahara! Who destroyed Manmadha is micro as well as macro?

iii) Salutations to Trinetra! Who existed before the beginning of creation and is ever youthful?

iv) Salutations to the Lord who is existing in everything and who is also immutable.

v) The Lord is the cause of the visible world and the origin of Maya (illusionary power). I bow down and offer my prayer.

With such contrasting descriptions (described in scriptures also) I am confused to find the truth and implications thereof. I therefore offer my Namaskāras to the Saguṇa and Nirguṇa forms of the Lord and seek pardon.

29 (b) Explanation as applicable to Viṣṇu:

The same explanation can be applied in favor of Viṣṇu.

The following salutary words may be added.

i) Priyadava: the destroyer of mundane a pleasure by vairagya (dispassion).

ii) Sṁarahara: Who eradicates the attraction from objects, for pursuing Bhakti to the deity.

iii) Trinayana: The Lord who acts as an eye to the three worlds and illuminate them and make them visible.

Verse 30

बहुल-रजसे विश्वोत्पत्तौ भवाय नमो नमः
प्रबल-तमसे तत् संहारे हराय नमो नमः।
जन-सुखकृते सत्त्वोद्रिक्तौ मृडाय नमो नमः
प्रमहसि पदे निस्त्रैगुण्ये शिवाय नमो नमः॥ ३०॥

bahula-rajase viśvotpattau bhavāya namo namaḥ
prabala-tamase tat saṁhāre harāya namo namaḥ |
jana-sukhakṛte sattvodriktau mṛḍāya namo namaḥ
prāmahasi pade nistraiguṇye śivāya namo namaḥ || 30 ||

30 (a) Meaning and Explanation:

O Deva Deva! I offer my Namaskar to, who has created as Brahma all the animate (with consciousness) and the inanimate objects in this world becoming a personification of Rajo guṇa.

I offer my Namaskār to, who as Viṣṇu blessed this world with your Sattva guṇa, the attribute of compassion and kindness.

I offer my Namaskār to, who as Rudra becoming a personification of Tamo guṇa, the attribute of darkness, where Tamas pervades for its destruction.

I offer my Namaskār to you Śiva! Who is beyond the guṇas and who takes one form or other at will. Being the supreme of the deities, a mass of self-effulgence, who created Maya but is beyond Maya, and being the cause of the final beatitude (mokṣa).

Each of the deity of the trinity has different attitude depending upon the predominance of one of three Guṇas.

30 (b) The explanation as applicable to Śiva is also applicable in favor of Viṣṇu.

Verse 31

कृश-परिणति-चेतः क्लेशवश्यं क्व चेदं
क्व च तव गुण-सीमोल्लङ्घिनी शश्वदृद्धिः।
इति चकितममन्दीकृत्य मां भक्तिराधाद्
वरद चरणयोस्ते वाक्य-पुष्पोपहारम्॥ ३१॥

kṛśa-pariṇati-cetaḥ kleśavaśyaṁ kva cedaṁ
kva ca tava guṇa-sīmollaṅghinī śaśvadṛddhiḥ |
iti cakitamamandīkṛtya māṁ bhaktirādhād
varada caraṇayoste vākya-puṣpopahāram || 31 ||

31 (a) Meaning and Explanation:

Puṣpadanta offered prayer as follows.

O Varada! You are the giver of blessings and fulfill all the desires of your devotees.

I have very meager knowledge and my mind is polluted by various kinds of afflictions due to entanglement in mundane desires and matters and consider myself incapable.

You are the supreme deity who transcend the three guṇas, one with limitless powers, very scared and self-efflugence. Thus, there is an incomparable contrast between us and therefore I am afraid. But my devotion to you has given me courage to procced with my worship. I humbly offer the vocal praises as lotus flowers at your feet. I humbly pray to accept my worship and pardon my mistakes.

Note: The original stotra inscribed at Amaralingeswara temple has only thirty-one slokas.

Madhusūdana Sarasvati has also written commentary for these thirty-one slokas.

The remaining stotras are considered as Phala Sruti which is usual for all prayer slokas giving the significance and fruits for reciting the slokas. Hence, the meaning and explanation as applicable to Viṣṇu has not been written.

Verse 32

अमित-गिरि-समं स्यात् कज्जलं सिन्धु-पात्रे
सुर-तरुवर-शाखा लेखनी पत्रमुर्वी।
लिखति यदि गृहीत्वा शारदा सर्वकालं
तदपि तव गुणानामीश पारं न याति॥ ३२॥

aSīta-giri-samaṁ syātkajjalaṁ sindhu-pātre
sura-taruvara-śākhā lekhanī patramurvī |
likhati yadi gṛhītvā śāradā sarvakālaṁ
tadapi tava guṇānāmīśa pāraṁ na yāti || 32 ||

32. Meaning and Explanation:

O Maheśwaran! In the manifest form you have immense delectable divine qualities. If the Goddess of learning Sarasvati would write forever without letup, using the blackness from Mount Anjana as ink, the ocean as an ink pot, the branch of the holy tree Kalpatarua as a quill, and the earth as a sheet, she would not be completing till the eternal time.

One can understand from the above that the divine qualities are immense beyond imagination or comprehension.

Verse 33

असुर-सुर-मुनीन्द्रैरर्चितस्येन्दु-मौलेः
ग्रथित-गुणमहिम्नो निर्गुणस्येश्वरस्य।
सकल-गण-वरिष्ठः पुष्पदन्ताभिधानः
रुचिरमलघुवृत्तैः स्तोत्रमेतच्चकार॥ ३३॥

asura-sura-munīndrairarcitasyendu-mauleḥ
grathita-guṇamahiṁno nirguṇasyeśvarasya |
sakala-guṇa-variṣṭhaḥ puṣpadantābhidhānaḥ
rucirāmalaghu vṛttaiḥ stotrametaccakāra || 33 ||

33. Meaning and Explanation:

The praise of the greatness and magnificence of Lord Śiva, Chandrasekhara, in the form as Chandrasmouli (who is wearing the crescent moon on his head) who is being worshipped by all the sages, devatās and demons was described in poetic form by the Puṣpadanta, the emperor of Gandharvas in sweet Sanskrit language in Sikharī chandas (metre).

Verse 34

अहरहरनवद्यं धूर्जटेः स्तोत्रमेतत्
पठति परमभक्त्या शुद्ध-चित्तः पुमान् यः।
स भवति शिवलोके रुद्रतुल्यस्तथाऽत्र
प्रचुरतर-धनायुः पुत्रवान् कीर्तिमांश्च॥ ३४॥

aharaharanavadyaṁ dhūrjaṭeḥ stotrametat
Tatpaṭhati paramabhaktyā śuddha-cittaḥ pumānyaḥ |
sa bhavati śivaloke rudratulyastdathā'tra
pracuratara-dhanāyuḥ putravān kīrtimāṁśca || 34 ||

34. Meaning and Explanation:

All those who, with ardent devotion with a clear conscience recites this stotra everyday, they would be blessed with abundance of health, long life, virtuous progeny and fame in this life and proximity with Supreme Being in the other world. This stotra is being chanted every day in the Himalayas due to the greatest significance of the stotra to Lord Siva.

Verse 35

महेशान्नापरो देवो महिम्नो नापरा स्तुतिः।
अघोरान्नापरो मन्त्रो नास्ति तत्त्वं गुरोः परम्॥ ३५॥

maheśānnāparo devo mahiṁno nāparā stutiḥ |
aghorānnāparo mantro nāsti tattvaṁ guroḥ param ||35 ||

35. Meaning and Explanation:

The deity Śiva is incomparable and there is none greater than Him. There is no song or hymn which is greater than Mahiṁna stavam. There is no mantra greater than Aghora mantra. There is no tattva or principle other than that of a venerable preceptor or guru.

A similar stotra was found in the Parasambhu Mahiṁna stavam composed by sage Dūrvāsa. '*Nasti tattvaṁ Guruho param*"

There are four steps in trying to reach the Supreme God. (i) A guru who will properly guide. (ii) Daily worship and chanting of holy names and stotra (iii) A mantra for meditation. (iv) An idol or rūpa of the deity.

Verse 36

दीक्षा दानं तपस्तीर्थं ज्ञानं यागादिकाः क्रियाः।
महिम्नस्तव पाठस्य कलां नार्हन्ति षोडशीम्॥ ३६॥

dīkṣā dānaṁ tapastīrthaṁ jñānaṁ yāgādikāḥ kriyāḥ |
mahiṁnastava pāṭhasya kalāṁ nārhanti ṣoḍaśīm ||36||

36. Meaning and Explanation.

i) If a ritual like yagna is contemplated, one must take a vow and follow certain prescribed order of life till the contemplated yagna is successfully performed is called deeksha.

ii) Dana is giving gifts or as alms to poor people out of compassion for them.

iii) Tapas means penance observing rigorous conditions till the objective is achieved. Usually for the blessing of the God.

iv) Teertha: to go on pilgrimage to holy places and bathing in holy rivers and having darśan of the deity of those places.

All these are advised for people to be performed to get purified and seeking blessings of the deities in the process of spiritual process by ordinary people and they will get peace of mind and virtuous qualities and inclination to undertake spiritual practice. The benefits accrued by all these will be less than one sixteenth value of the value of benefit obtained by reciting of Mahiṁnastotra. Thus, the greatness of the Mahimnastotra is highlighted.

Verse 37

कुसुमदशन-नामा सर्व-गन्धर्व-राजः
शशिधरवर-मौलेर्देवदेवस्य दासः।
स खलु निज-महिम्नो भ्रष्ट एवास्य रोषात्
स्तवनमिदमकार्षीद् दिव्य-दिव्यं महिम्नः॥ ३७॥

kusumadaśana-nāmā sarva-gandharva-rājaḥ
śaśidharavara-maulerdevadevasya dāsaḥ |
sa khalu nija-mahiṁno bhraṣṭa evāsya roṣāt
stavanamidamakārṣīd divya-divyaṁ mahiṁnaḥ || 37 ||

37. Meaning and explanation.

The king of Gandharva, named Puṣpadanta who has lost his powers as Gandharva due to incurring of wrath of God for a sin committed by him inadvertently. That very moment, he realized that some mistake was committed and instantaneously started praise of the Lord Śiva who is supreme deity and who is wearing crescent moon on his head. and seeking pardon for his sinful deed. Lord Śiva was pleased with the sincere and humble prayer of the devotee and restored Gandharva powers to Puṣpadanta.

The stotra has adequately shown the attitude with which one should be devoted to the Lord. One should have the purity of mind, sincerity and humbleness in behavior and faith and devotion. The realization of committing a mistake or acceptance of guilt and seeking pardon are also essential.

Verse 38

सुरगुरुमभिपूज्य स्वर्ग-मोक्षैक-हेतुं
पठति यदि मनुष्यः प्राञ्जलिर्नान्य-चेताः।
व्रजति शिव-समीपं किन्नरैः स्तूयमानः
स्तवनमिदममोघं पुष्पदन्तप्रणीतम्॥ ३८॥

suragurumabhipūjya svarga-mokṣaika-hetuṁ
paṭhati yadi manuṣyaḥ prāñjalirnānya-cetāḥ |
vrajati śiva-samīpaṁ kinnaraiḥ stūyamānaḥ
stavanamidamamoghaṁ puṣpadantapraṇītam || 38 ||

38. Meaning and Explanation:

This stotra or hymn of praise of Śiva by Puṣpadant which is extolled by pious sages and seers, worthy of respect by demi Gods, and demons and also by human beings, which can achieve the heaven or final beatitude (mokṣa). If anyone with folded hands before (or imagining the presence of) the Lord with whole hearted (with body, mind and soul) devotion recites this Stava they will be taken to the proximity of Śiva honored with the escort by celestial kinnaras.

Thus the great significance of and fruits of reciting the praise of the Lord Śiva is once again stated.

Verse 39

आसमाप्तमिदं स्तोत्रं पुण्यं गन्धर्व-भाषितम्।
अनौपम्यं मनोहारि सर्वमीश्वरवर्णनम्॥ ३९॥

āsamāptamidaṁ stotraṁ puṇyaṁ gandharva-bhāṣitam |
anaupamyaṁ manohāri sarvamīśvaravarṇanam || 39 ||

39. Meaning and Explanation:

This stotra which is beautiful and full of devotion to Śiva, the bestower of auspiciousness was composed from beginning till the end in a fascinating manner.

Thus Puṣpadant indicated that he feels this is the appropriate stotra to Śiva.

Verse 40

इत्येषा वाङ्मयी पूजा श्रीमच्छङ्कर-पादयोः।
अर्पिता तेन देवेशः प्रीयतां मे सदाशिवः॥ ४०॥

ityeṣā vāṅmayī pūjā śrīmacchaṅkara-pādayoḥ |
arpitā tena deveśaḥ prīyatāṁ me sadāśivaḥ || 40 ||

40. Meaning and Explanation:

This Mahiṁna stotra in the form of vocal presentation is offered as flowers at the lotus feet of Śiva who is the Supreme among the deities. May my Iṣṭa devata (most cherished deity) Śiva be pleased. Thus Puṣpadant offered prayers to Śiva.

Verse 41

तव तत्त्वं न जानामि कीदृशोऽसि महेश्वर।
यादृशोऽसि महादेव तादृशाय नमो नमः॥ ४१॥

tava tattvaṁ na jānāmi kīdṛśo’si maheśvara |
yādṛśo’si mahādeva tādṛśāya namo namaḥ || 41 ||

41. Meaning and Explanation:

Puṣpadant addressed Śiva humbly submitting that he is ignorant about the greatness and Truth of the Lord's qualities. It is beyond the scope of people like me. I can only offer my prayers to your true self.

Verse 42

एककालं द्विकालं वा त्रिकालं यः पठेन्नरः।
सर्वपाप-विनिर्मुक्तः शिव लोके महीयते॥ ४२॥

ekakālaṁ dvikālaṁ vā trikālaṁ yaḥ paṭhennaraḥ |
sarvapāpa-vinirmuktaḥ śiva loke mahīyate || 42 ||

42. Meaning and Explanation:

This Mahimnastotra, if recited every day either once, twice or three times by any person , he will be absolved of all sins and revels in Śiva loka after the fall of his body

Verse 43

श्री पुष्पदन्त-मुख-पङ्कज-निर्गतेन
स्तोत्रेण किल्बिष-हरेण हर-प्रियेण।
कण्ठस्थितेन पठितेन समाहितेन
सुप्रीणितो भवति भूतपतिर्महेशः॥ ४३॥

śrī puṣpadanta-mukha-paṅkaja-nirgatena
stotreṇa kilbiṣa-hareṇa hara-priyeṇa |
kaṇṭhasthitena paṭhitena samāhitena
suprīṇito bhavati bhūtapatirmaheśaḥ || 43 ||

43. Meaning and Explanation:

This Mahiṁna stotra has flowed from the lotus mouth of Puṣpadant. A person who ever gets this by heart, or recites or even preserves it at home as a sacred book, the lord of all, Maheswara will be pleased and they can secure His blessings.

॥ इति श्री पुष्पदन्त विरचितं शिवमहिम्नः स्तोत्रं समाप्तम्॥

|| iti śrī puṣpadanta viracitaṁ śivamahimnaḥ stotraṁ samāptam ||

Thus ends the Śiva Mahiṁna stotra composed by Puṣpadant.